My Father's
PRAYER

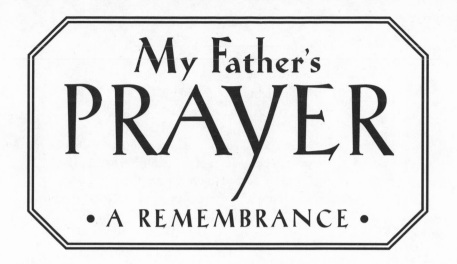

My Father's PRAYER

• A REMEMBRANCE •

Phyllis Tickle

UPPER
ROOM BOOKS
NASHVILLE

My Father's Prayer

Cover Design: Bruce Gore
Cover Photograph: © Tad Stamm/Picturesque
Interior Design: Jim Bateman
First Printing: April 1995 (7)
ISBN: 0-8358-0733-9
Library of Congress Catalog Number: 94-61264

Printed in the United States of America

THIS BOOK
Is dedicated to the memory of
Laura Simpson,
a dark friend;

Was joyfully written for Snab,
whose book it always was;

Has been, from the beginning, a gift for Dunlap
and his cousins.

It was the winter of 1937,

the deep dark winter of 1937, and I was almost four. Still three, but almost four. Even I knew that, in the all-engulfing, all-incorporating way of children when they deal with history or time. And there was war in Europe. I knew that too, but I knew it in a detached way.

War was a fact somewhere in my parents' conversation. It was a circumstance wrapped so snugly in the shades of their evening talk that I could not make of it a familiar thing. I could not even snatch a decent glimpse of it as it fled from the probe of my questions. But it was there. That is, it was there until it came to dinner one night.

9

There was an early twilight that evening. The first
hard freezes had already wilted and burned away
the last of my autumn pleasures and confined me,
rebellious and offended, to the dim interiors of our
campus apartment. Like all mountain houses, ours
too would be gray and unmappable in its duskiness
until a thick lay of snow would come outside the
windows, bringing us its reflected light. But I had
known this sorrow before. I had learned to wait for
the snow and the winter's sharp, crisp light flooding
the playroom floor, and the cold joy of my swing in
the snowlight, and the blur of my sled rushing down
the hill behind the history building, and the laughter
of the undergraduates as they snowballed each other
and sometimes me, and sometimes . . . although they
always claimed it as accidental . . . sometimes my
professor father.

10

I knew these things, but I did not know about phone calls yet, not phone calls at the dinner hour in those lost years when the dinner hour was eucharistic for those of us who gathered to it and held inviolate even by those who did not.

My mother's pre-World War II phone was of the newest design and one of the few vanities I can ever remember her having invested in. Mother's phone sat. In other words, it did not hang, glued to an oak panel and bracketed to the wall like most, nor did it require cranking in order to work. Black and pristine, her phone arose from its sleek round base with only half a body, or so it seemed to me. Only one arm hung from only one shoulder, but its mouth was beautiful, flared and trumpeting and almost always still warm from her conversations when I touched it.

11

When her phone rang that night at so unseemly and indecorous an hour, my mother waited, as was proper, for my father to excuse himself from the table to the living room and the whirring call.

❧ ❧

12

*I cannot remember now
how he told her or how they
told me or even if they did.*

Perhaps I gathered. That too is the way of children. By whatever means, however, I came, before full nightfall, to understand that war had taken on a new and more immediate position in our lives. My uncle's ship had been sunk at sea . . . torpedoed by the Germans in the Atlantic trade routes just off the Azores.

15

I remember only my father's words, "He shouldn't have tried it! I knew he should not have tried it!" and my mother sitting at the table, her chair pushed back from her place and the picture frame from her dressing table clutched in her left hand. I remember how white her hands were and how her bracelet broke light across the candlelit cloth. I remember that she did not cry, only that she stared through the window at the obscuring cold.

Young and lean, as dark of eyes and hair as she herself was, my uncle, her youngest brother, stared at me through her fingers. The chin below his Porter nose cast a fine, patrician shadow over the Merchant Marine uniform he was wearing. As if to counterbalance the chin, he had set the brim of his dress hat so that it too would cast a shadow, a vague one, over his high left cheek. I loved him.

It would be another ten years before I would begin to use correctly words like *contraband cargo* and *ammunitions* and *underground* and *resistance. Nazism* and *Mein Kampf* and *Il Duce* were lost on one so

young and so secured; but not on the dashing young
uncle who sailed the Atlantic seaways for his living
and sent me postcards from half a dozen ports. Nor
were they lost on my parents who had lived abroad
for a year to two while my father studied European
instructional systems and methodology. Such things
were not lost on them.

In time, that marvelously healing capsule in which
we all are nurtured to a strength will sustain us
outside of it. . . .

In time, the telephone would ring again, but it
would be morning and I would be still half-wrapped
in blanket dreams. I would hear my mother weep at
last, the sound coming across the transom between
my room and theirs; but her release would be dressed

17

in my father's deeper laughter and I would
understand in some unspoken way that the uncle
had been rescued. Lacking any clear idea of the life
of the sea, I would also lack any clear idea of what
that meant. For years I would rather fancy the
uncle as riding gaily into the port of Lisbon astride
a Disney dolphin, his Porter chin still unscathed and
the snap-brim dress hat still casting its shadow on his
high left cheek.

*After that, of course,
war came closer.*

We sat out the twilights of my fourth year in the living room by the new wireless. All over the world, dining room evenings with their fair linen and candles were fading away, and we were no exception.

Apart from the thrumming glow of the new radio's bulbous tubes, there was no light in the late afternoons where we sat as a family in my mother's parlor and listened to the sounds of a dying order. It was to me as if the parents were afraid somehow of those exquisite lamps, afraid that their soft glow might chase away the wireless's sound; might warm the corners of the room and sap the intensity of their

21

focus; might add comfort where only despair was
intense enough to support us.

Eventually the Rock of Gibraltar's station was the
last free voice still coming out of Europe. Clinging
to that ancient Pillar of Hercules like those lashed
against the terrors of a roiling sea, the outpost and
those who broadcast from it crackled for months
across an ocean and into our apartment before the
winter afternoon when they were no more. I watched
as my father, his fingers more tremulous with each
spin of his dials, adjusted and tuned and corrected,
all to no avail. Gibraltar was gone.

I saw my father cry for the first time that afternoon.
He sat in the shadowing room, his arms crossed as
if in self-embrace, and his tears were crooked little

22

streams down his stone-cast face. He had fought in
the First War, an expert in cryptology and telegraphy.
The loss of Gibraltar meant another war. He was too
old to go, too young to watch. In the place of both,
he wept.

❧ ❧

The official declarations of war
came shortly thereafter,

just as he had known they would, and with them the hateful air-raid drills. Hours . . . or so it seemed to me then . . . under the dining room table, Mother's drapes sealed with ugly paper tape hard against the window facings and no light anywhere . . . hours when my father, a block warden, patrolled unarmed and checking . . . hours when the silence was an exquisite thirst for any sound, but especially for that of the all-clear and his key in the door again.

Within a year after that, the trips began. I did not know why and I almost never knew where, only that he was gone and that when he returned his luggage

27

was more filled with papers and taped-shut folders than with his clothes and linen. I remember that once, when he was unpacking, a darling little lizard slithered frantically from amongst his papers and across the bedroom floor. I had never seen such a creature before and was as enchanted as my mother was offended.

28

So soon as the creature and Mother's consternation were both soothed, only my wonder remained . . . my wonder and some vague recognition that the suitcase had been to a distant place far beyond the range of the flowers and trees and creatures that I knew so personally and so intricately.

Desert! It was a dangerous word. The lizard frantic in my old fish bowl faded into all the lizards in my

Child's Book of Wonder. Desert. My father had been to a place like the *Book of Wonder*'s desert. Willie (for I had named him almost immediately) died at some forgotten moment and departed this life unmourned. By the time of his death, even his exoticism had paled into nothingness compared to my father's.

29

The years did pass,

as even years of agony tend mercifully to do. Late phone calls and desert trips, air-raid drills and practiced blackouts, dark-hatted men at the front door and long hours behind other (and closed) doors . . . they all receded from our lives again. War was once more a monster appeased. Grumbling and not yet sated, it was at least dormant enough so that most of us who had been innocent in 1937 could grow up.

33

In time, that vessel whose walls are marked and measured, graduated and imprinted by our memory . . . in time, I would come upon some consistency, some centralizing sanity, some motif that, if it did not make sense of those years of scarred childhood and of the ones that followed it, did at least make some order out of them. And I was to find that sanctuary in the memory of my father's hands.

*In retrospect I know that the
education of my soul*

began sometime close to midnight on the night of that unnatural phone call with its messages of terror at sea. Sometime during the late evening hours lost to me now in no-recall, I had been put to bed. But if I cannot remember my going, I can vividly remember my rousing . . . the pounding in my breathways . . . the gasping cold of the floor beneath my bare feet . . . and the urgency which drove me to endure it in order to reach the safety of my parents' room.

The feral dark which had come to our dining room windows earlier and permitted my mother the comfort of its deceptive blankness was no longer

safely outside the windows. Sometime during
the hours I had slept, it had insinuated itself like a
miasma through the cracks in the casings and the
draughts in the frames. It lay now, a furred other-life,
between me and the glow of activity seeping in from
around the closed door.

In my terror to shoot through the darkness before
it could realize and engulf me, I more burst through
than opened the door adjoining the two bedrooms,
yet neither of my parents seemed to hear me. My
mother lay, sleeping at last, in her single bed. My
father, still dressed as at dinner, sat beside his larger,
double one with only his tie loosened. He had pulled
Mother's armless rocker, the one she called her
sewing chair and which she always set by the window
when she did her needlework, up close to the bed's

38

edge. There he sat, hunched slightly forward over
the bed's expanse with his massive shoulders curved
slightly forward in concentration on something in
front of him.

Mother's black, Chinese-lacquer workbasket was
beside him on the bed, and at his feet was the tissue-
lined box of yarn rosettes she had been weaving
since late summer. Mesmerized by the incongruity
of the delicate rosettes and the huge blunt fingers,
I watched as my father lifted up yet another wool
rosette from its place in the cardboard box; set it
tentatively at several different places along the
patchwork of rosettes he was making; finally selected
a place and began, crochet hook in his hand, to
secure the newcomer into the pattern which lay,
eight or nine rosettes long and in places three or four

39

rosettes deep, in front of him.

"Did Mama teach you to do that?" I blurted the words, so great was my astonishment, but he seemed not to hear them as an impertinence. Indeed, if anything, he seemed more surprised by my presence than distressed by my rudeness.

40

"No," he said, "my mama did, years ago," and the hook flashed again.

"I never saw you do it before."

"More's the pity," he said. Then he added, more to himself than to me, "But perhaps I never needed it before."

"Does Mama know you're doing it?" Permission was hard to come by at our house. I was already old enough to know that all too well; and I could no more have prevented the question than I could have stopped the terrors of my night from embracing me.

"Yes."

He didn't look up from his work, but I could see the half-smile which always started, when he was amused, at the cleft beneath his nose and spread across his thin lips until it met again just above the crevice of his chin. Thus emboldened, I moved closer to him.

"And she doesn't care?" I was as much impressed as amazed at this point.

41

"Yes, but she doesn't object."

I went back to bed, forgetful of whatever my mission
had been, of whatever demons had beleaguered me,
of whatever urgency had threatened me. And even
though the morning brought my mother's tears of
relief and my father's healing laughter to rouse me,
the events of that pivotal evening were never
destined to be contained within it. Instead, they
were to spread like a secret mesh of vine and verdure
across a lifetime.

42

*The rosette coverlet—for that
is what it was eventually
to become—*

grew in my father's hands for all the years that stretched from the winter of 1937 to the horror of Hiroshima. Night after night, at evening's end, while the wireless tubes faded and cooled in the darkened living room, he would pour a glass of milk, make himself a plate of cheese and crackers, and move from the kitchen into the bedroom. There, drawing the armless rocker up beside his bed, he would sit and work.

Some nights he simply wove rosettes from the scraps and hanks of wool yarn which it was increasingly difficult for Mother and her friends to locate and bring home to him. Some nights—ones, I know now, when he felt some shaft of hope piercing our mountain dark—he patterned the coverlet, assigning and then incorporating rosettes he had already woven. As the War progressed, Mother began to join him.

On the nights when they worked together, it was Mother who sat in the rocker while he hooked or wove, precariously perched on the edge of his bed. Bed-setting was another prohibition that was stringently enforced at our house, and my father's obvious license to violate it amazed more than a few of my childish evenings. But even in those shared times of two parental heads bent and two sets of parental hands busied, the rosettes were my father's work.

Although it was she who had begun the project,
my mother never touched the coverlet again, except
to admire it with him. She occupied herself instead
with the ugly—or so I thought—khaki yarns that
were issued to her every month by the Red Cross and
from which she (and all the other women who knew
how) were expected to knit heavy wool hosiery for
Allied boots.

As the maw of war swallowed up year after colorless
year, as the evenings of air drills and the days of
rationing lines became, by their very repetitiousness,
more and more burdensome, so the pre-sleep hours in
the bedroom seemed too to increase, coming earlier
and earlier into our night's activities. Like monastics
of any faith who dream of surcease as they move to
their prayers, so my parents moved toward that

47

consoling space. There the salmon-tinted bulbs of
Mother's wall scones suffused the last vestiges of a
lost decadence across the litany of their hands,
making benediction out of shadows and familiarity.
And there, before war's end, all the metaphors of
religion were to be brought home to my young soul
and given parental permission to flourish within me.

For months while it was growing,

the rosette coverlet was stored each night, as were all works in progress, in Mother's cedar storage chest. As the War dragged on and the coverlet grew, it became too bulky for the chest, and my father was forced to leave it, large but still unfinished, spread out on his bed.

By the spring of my eleventh year when Normandy's beaches had been successfully stormed and fear was a less ready guest, my mother had taken to quipping that if the War did not end soon, the coverlet would exceed even the reaches of the bed. My father was obviously pleased by her decreasing anxiety and smiled that thin half-smile of his whenever she

twitted him; but he was not to be dissuaded. His
weaving and sewing no longer had anything to do
either with craft or with the coverlet. They had,
instead, become a discipline, and we all knew it.

Each stitch securing the petals of a rosette, each
thread woven to fill in a center, each loop catching
one into pattern . . . every individual flash of needle
or hook, in fact . . . had been translated over the slow
years into tangible prayer. So long as he stitched, my
father kept the faith with those who could not—kept
it until, as he so biblically said, "this indignation be
overpast."

By V-J Day, when he tied off his last stitch, the
rosettes had indeed grown to cover the bed literally
from the floor on one side to the floor on the other

52

side and from the floor at the bed's foot to the edge of its head, back again to cover the doubled pillows and then up, over, and back around them. He had kept the faith.

My father never shaped another rosette after that, and, so far as I know, he never picked up another needle or held another thread again, except as an incidental act born of a connoisseur's affection. He contented himself instead with buying huge quantities of stamped linen and fine damasks for Mother, and elaborate canvasses for petit point that she hated and he always wished her to enjoy.

53

᪣᪣

As for his part,
my father turned,

at war's end, from needlecraft to wildflowers, because there was at last gasoline enough to allow him to roam our mountains in pursuit of them; and to painting, because he so admired Mr. Churchill and because he found in the Prime Minister's defense of the amateur painter a rhetoric he wished to support. Yet the painting he took up was not the Churchillian temerity of colors splashed against a naked canvas. Rather, my father began to tint by hand and with incredible delicacy the photographs he had taught himself to take with the new, post-War box cameras.

As with his wildflowers, by eliciting shadow and light

57

where none was, he created simple beauties with
no claim to any accolade beyond joy, both his in
the doing and the viewer's in the seeing. In all
those years of war, he said, he had learned well
the humility of the needle and of those who build
with it.

58

Midway of my childhood,

we moved from our campus quarters to ones of our own in town. The new old house was selected, in no small part, for the excellence of its secluded and sunny gardens and for the brilliant lighting of its workroom. There the quiet intensity of the old rosettes became the illuminated intensity of the new pointillized photographs, and the perfumes of Mother's cedar chest became the more fulsome ones of turned earth and mountain loam. We had come full circle, back to memory's earliest days, back to sunlit joys and evening pleasures.

But I who had learned by then to stitch and knit and

61

hook with skill, lacked my father's gift with either oils or plants; I was forced to join those restored hours of afternoon delights as an observer rather than as an apprentice to his wonders. It was a bitter time for me, and its longings still bite deeply into my appreciation of both his exquisite tints and his flower beds.

62

I asked him once (and only once) in the forgivable way of young adolescents, why he never stitched anymore. It was midsummer and we were in the shaded beds where he grew his trilliums and Solomon's seals. He didn't say anything at first, just trowelled on for a minute or two. When he did look up, there was a mist in his eyes, a gathering of memory in the corners, which I have never forgotten.

He set his clump of plants down and studied me intently. I understood in that moment that he was gauging my years and tallying carefully how far I might have come in their brevity. "The coverlet is in me now," he said. "I don't need to make another one. Can you understand that?"

"Yes, sir." And in some numb, diffuse way it was true. I did.

Reassured either by my answer or by its surrogate of my earnestness, he returned to his transplanting. "Besides," he said, his voice directed more at the dark earth he had just turned than at me, "I haven't stopped really. I'm still stitching, just in other ways."

The July heat, normally moist and oppressive in the

63

mountains by that time of afternoon, was transparent and warm around us like the affection of near kin. I can remember being conscious of the fact that even the apple trees had stopped leafing and chattering, and of the fact that I did not want to be distracted from my father's words by the abnormality of their silence.

64

"My mother was a piece of needlework," he said finally. His words had a kind of soft distance that made them more a logical sequel to his thoughts than a non sequitur in the conversation. "Maybe we all are in some ways. God knows we use enough of the language, don't we? . . . explaining ourselves to ourselves . . . 'hemming a fellow in' . . . 'knitting a family together' . . . 'spinning a yarn' . . . 'cutting the strings' . . . ." He chuckled at his own chain of figures. "Metaphors," he said. "All metaphors, but what would we ever do without them?"

He tamped dirt around the clump of lady slippers he had just finished setting. "You're a lot like my mother—loving with a needle the way she was— but she always said that real needlework took a tough spirit as well." He cut his eyes up at me. I remember being chilled then, as if by some fear of what he already knew and that I had still to learn. "Being willing to decorate the ordinary with the perishable requires courage, you know . . . the same kind of courage as living does."

He sat back on his heels and reconsidered the lady slippers. They were a constant frustration to him, for they resisted to their own deaths his repeated

65

attempts to move them from their natal elevations
in the hills to our lower valley. Regardless of how
many sortees he made into the range which encircled
us and regardless of how many yards of slippers he
brought back with him, he could never manage to
sustain any profusion of them. I was afraid for a
minute that he would forget me in his absorption
with the recalcitrant transplants. The apple trees
and I waited together.

He stood up and brushed the grains of rotted wood
dirt off his pants legs. "I thought a lot about my
mother while I was working the coverlet. Did you
know that?"

This time I had no need to feign. I had indeed
known that. I nodded.

"She used to say that she could tell what a piece of work had taught someone and who it was that had been willing to learn." The thin smile spread around the corners of his lips and rippled on toward its center above his chin. "I wondered what she would have said about the coverlet and me."

"Did it teach you anything?" Even though the innocence of the wildflowers and the silence of the apple trees had given me permission, his mood was still broken, yanked back from reverie to reportage.

"Yes, of course, it did." He was impatient of his answer if not of my question. "All of those things you would suppose from a long, complicated project like that . . ."

67

Then his eyes drifted off of me again for just a moment and he said, "But mainly the coverlet showed me how it was—in what way it was, that is—that Mama was right. Stitches do take the time they are made in and spend it to change the people who are making them." His voice was hesitant and slightly higher than usual as if he were both tentative of his commentary and relieved to have found it. "Always remember that I told you that, Princess. Watch the people as much as their stitches." I always did.

68

When he died
thirty-five years later,

my father was still sleeping under the rosette coverlet. I was with him when he finally slipped away, and he went calling for his mother. After the funeral, Mother burned the rosette coverlet. It was the only way she knew to send it to him and we could not bear, either of us, to think of him without it.

71

Epilogue

All appearances to the contrary, this is not a book about cottage handiwork and the domestic crafts, or at least it is not a book about them as such. Nor is it a book about my father really, though certainly it has been written in gratitude to him.

No, instead this book is about a space interior to us all and about how he taught me to go there . . . about that space where what we think and what we do can sit a while and be at peace with each other. This book is about that place where the center holds, and the world external to it is for a moment stilled.

When hands and thoughts are occupied in the
goodness of small and needful creation, the spirit
rests that deep rest in which it can attend itself
and be attended by the sacred. Distrustful always
of the time and circumstance entwined in human
perceptions, my father spoke with his attention the
established prayers of the psalms and the church and
tradition; but he sent his spirit, refreshed and whole,
when he would speak as himself to God. The result,
like its motivation, was a singular reverence as well
as a simple gift that wanted passing along.

73

About the Author

Phyllis A. Tickle is Religion Editor of *Publishers Weekly*, the international journal of the book industry, and author of several books on religion and Christianity. Before assuming this position, she was for twenty years an editor and publisher of general interest books as well as a frequent contributor on religion to various national periodicals.

Among Tickle's published works by Upper Room Books are *What the Heart Already Knows, Ordinary Time,* and *Final Sanity.* Other books include *Tobias and the Angel, The City Essays,* and *American Genesis.*

Also, she has published poetry in many anthologies and journals. Prior to entering publishing, she was a fellow at Furman University, a lecturer at Rhodes College, and for a number of years, Dean of Humanities at The Memphis College of Art.

Tickle, who is a lector in the Episcopal Church, lives with her husband, Sam, in western Tennessee.